the
RAFFI
SINGABLE
SONGBOOK

A COLLECTION OF 51 SONGS
FROM RAFFI'S FIRST THREE RECORDS
FOR YOUNG CHILDREN

with illustrations by Joyce Yamamoto

CROWN PUBLISHERS, INC.   NEW YORK

For Debi

Published in the United States of America in 1987 by Crown Publishers, Inc., 225 Park Avenue South, New York, New York 10003
CROWN is a trademark of Crown Publishers, Inc.
Manufactured in Italy

Library of Congress Cataloging-in-Publication Data
Raffi. [Songs. Selections] The Raffi singable songbook. Summary: a noted Canadian recording artist presents his own songs. 1. Children's songs. [1. Songs] I. Yamamoto, Joyce, ill. II. Title.
M1997.R1726R3 1987   87-750289
ISBN 0-517-56637-0

10 9 8 7 6 5 4 3 2

INTRODUCTION

This songbook was made in response to many requests for sheet music of these recorded songs. Well, here it is — sheet music and a whole lot more.

Happy singing and playing!

- Raffi

ACKNOWLEDGEMENTS

David Tanner: Piano Arrangements

Joyce Yamamoto: Illustrations and Cover Design

Additional Illustrations by children from all over Canada

Photo Credits: Eedie Steiner, cover photo
Rudi Christl, page 49
Dorothy Harack, page 37
Kandice Abbot, page 59

    My thanks to Joyce Yamamoto for the long hours she spent on many aspects of this book — proofreading, layout, design, and of course the delightful illustrations that are definitely Joyce. Many thanks to David Tanner for his diligent work in arranging these recorded songs for piano with such care. And thanks to Ken Whiteley for his useful suggestions; to Bonnie and Bert Simpson for their advice; and to Debi for her help and loving support.

                            R.

Music engraving and typesetting by Musictype Limited, Goodwood, Ontario

Printed and bound by W. R. Draper, Weston, Ontario

CRAYON LEGEND

 SINGABLE SONGS FOR THE VERY YOUNG

MORE SINGABLE SONGS

 THE CORNER GROCERY STORE

CONTENTS

ALPHABETICAL INDEX

Aikendrum

March tempo

1. There was a man lived in the moon, in the moon, in the moon, there was a man lived in the moon and his name was Ai-ken-drum. 2. And he drum.

2. And he played upon a ladle, a ladle, a ladle,
He played upon a ladle and his name was Aikendrum.

3. And his hair was made of spaghetti . . .

4. And his eyes were made of meatballs . . .

5. And he played upon a ladle . . .

6. And his nose was made of cheese . . .

7. And his mouth was made of pizza . . .

8. And he played upon a ladle . . .

9. There was a man lived in the moon . . .

Anansi

Music by Raffi
Words by Bert Simpson

10

Baa, Baa, Black Sheep

BOOM BOOM!

Moderate

Chorus

Boom boom! ain't it great to be cra - zy, Boom boom! ain't it great to be cra - zy. Gid - dy and fool - ish all day long, Boom boom! ain't it great to be

Brush Your Teeth

Adapted and arranged by
Louise Dain and Raffi

2. When you wake up in the morning and it's quarter to two,
   And you want to find something to do, *Chorus*

3. When you wake up in the morning and it's quarter to three,
   And your mind starts humming twiddle de dee, *Chorus*

4. When you wake up in the morning and it's quarter to four,
   And you think you hear a knock on your door, *Chorus*

Bumping Up And Down

Traditional
Adapted by
Raffi and Ken Whiteley

2. One wheel's off and the axle's broken . . .
3. Freddie's gonna fix it with his hammer . . .
4. Bumping up and down in my little red wagon . . .

5. One wheel's off and the axle's broken . . .
6. Laura's gonna fix it with her pliers . . .
7. Bumping up and down in my little red wagon . . .

Cluck, Cluck, Red Hen

Music Traditional
Adapted lyrics by Jacquelyn Reinach

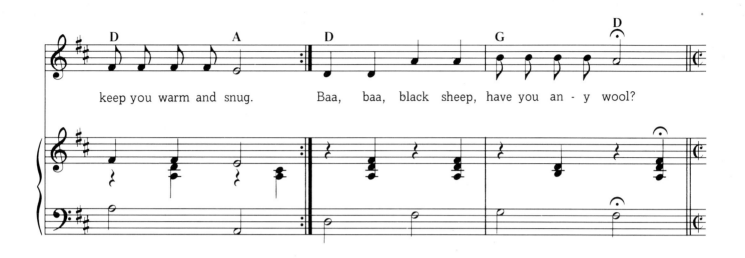

keep you warm and snug. Baa, baa, black sheep, have you an - y wool?

Faster

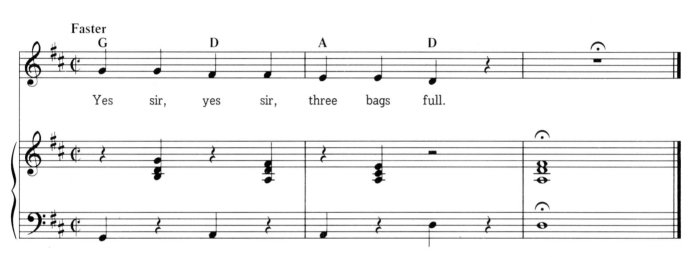

Yes sir, yes sir, three bags full.

2. Cluck, cluck, red hen, have you any eggs?
   Yes sir, yes sir, as many as your legs.
   One for your breakfast and one for your lunch,
   Come back tomorrow, I'll have another bunch.

3. Moo, moo, brown cow, have you milk for me?
   Yes sir, yes sir, as tasty as can be.
   Churn it into butter, make it into cheese,
   Freeze it into ice-cream or drink it if you please.

4. Buzz, buzz, busy bee, is your honey sweet?
   Yes sir, yes sir, sweet enough to eat.
   Honey on your muffin, honey on your cake,
   Honey by the spoonful, as much as I can make.

Comin' Down The Chimney

Music traditional
Adapted lyrics by Raffi

Slowly

Com - in' down the chim - ney   when he comes.

2. He'll be bringin' lots of goodies . . .

3. He'll have all of his reindeer . . .

4. And he'll need some milk and cookies . . .

5. He'll be comin' down the chimney . . .

The Corner Grocery Store

Music Traditional
Adapted lyrics by Raffi and Debi Pike

Medium

Verse

There was cheese, cheese, walk - in' on its knees, In the store, in the store. There was cheese, cheese, walk - in' on its knees, In the cor - ner gro - cer - y store. My

store. eyes are ___ dim, I can - not see, I

have not ___ brought my specs with me, I have not ___

brought my ___ specs with me. 2. There were

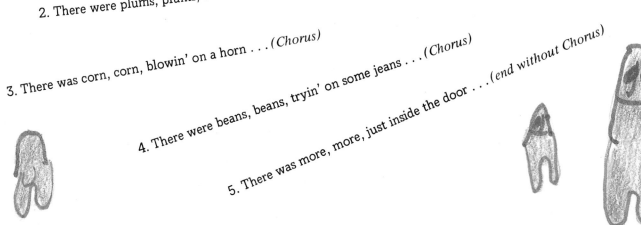

2. There were plums, plums, twiddling their thumbs . . . *(Chorus)*

3. There was corn, corn, blowin' on a horn . . . *(Chorus)*

4. There were beans, beans, tryin' on some jeans . . . *(Chorus)*

5. There was more, more, just inside the door . . . *(end without Chorus)*

Douglas Mountain

Music by Alec Wilder
Lyrics by Arnold Sundgaard

Snows are a-fall-in' on
Trim-min' the wicks on

Doug - las Moun - tain, Snows are a-fall in' so
Doug - las Moun - tain, Shin - in' my chim-ney so

Down By The Bay

Traditional

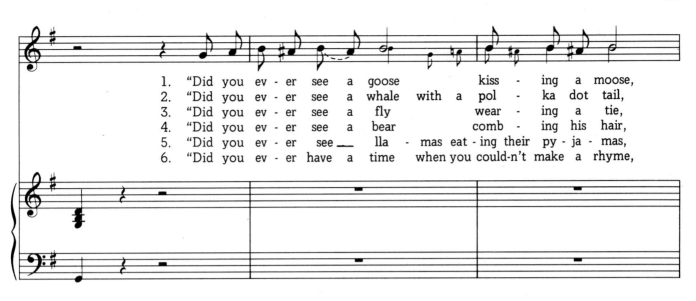

1. "Did you ev - er see a goose   kiss - ing a moose,
2. "Did you ev - er see a whale with a pol - ka dot tail,
3. "Did you ev - er see a fly   wear - ing a tie,
4. "Did you ev - er see a bear   comb - ing his hair,
5. "Did you ev - er see ___ lla - mas eat - ing their py - ja - mas,
6. "Did you ev - er have a time   when you could-n't make a rhyme,

WYNNE BILLEY

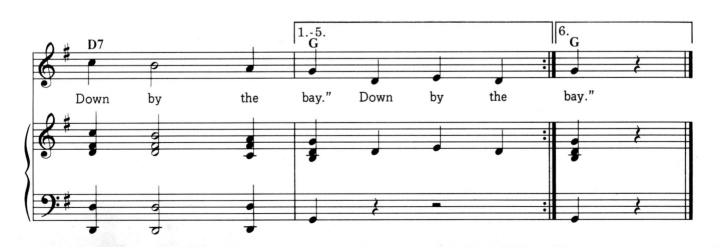

Down   by   the   bay."   Down   by   the   bay."

Five Little Frogs

(From: "Singing Fun")

By Lucille Wood/Louise Scott

Unaccompanied

Five green and speck - led frogs, sat on a speck - led log,

Eat - ing some most de - li - cious bugs. *(Yum yum)*

One jumped in - to the pool, where it was nice and cool,

Then there were four green speck - led frogs. *(gllb, gllb)*

Next verse: Four frogs, then Three, Two, One, "No green speckled frogs".

Five Little Pumpkins

A capella

Traditional

Five lit - tle pump - kins sit - ing on a gate.

First one said, "Oh my it's get - ting late." Sec - ond one said, "There are

witch - es in the air." The third one said, "But

we don't care." The fourth one said, "Let's run and run and run." The

fifth one said, "I'm read - y for some fun." "Oo oo," went the wind and

rit.

out went the light, And the five lit - tle pump - kins rolled out of sight.

Frère Jacques

Traditional

Frè - re Jac - ques, Frè - re Jac - ques, dor - mez vous? Dor - mez vous?

Son - nez les ma - tin - es, son - nez les ma - tin - es, ding dang dong, ding dang dong.

* Canon entry points.

Going On A Picnic

(From: "Singing Fun")

By Georgia E. Garlid/Lynn Freeman Olson

Go - ing on a pic - nic,

leav - ing right a - way. If it does - n't rain we'll stay all day.

Fine

Verse 2 repeat 4 times

Did you bring the sand - wich - es? Yes, I brought the sand - wich - es.
Did you bring the sal - ad? Yes, I brought the sal - ad.

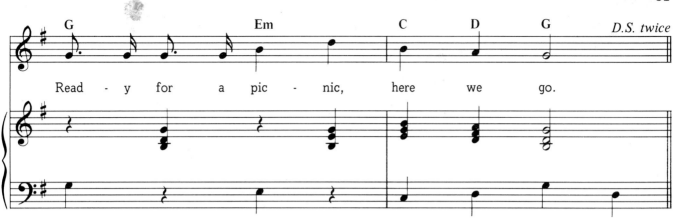

Read - y for a pic - nic, here we go.

2nd verse: Did you bring the melon?
Yes, I brought the melon.

Did you bring the apples?
Yes, I brought the apples.

Did you bring the lemonade?
Yes, I brought the lemonade.

Did you bring the cookies?
Yes, I brought the cookies.

Ready for a picnic,
Here we go.

Going To The Zoo

by Tom Paxton

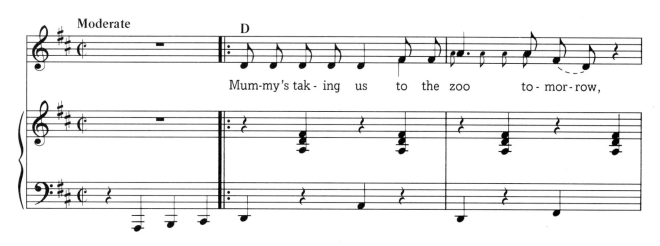

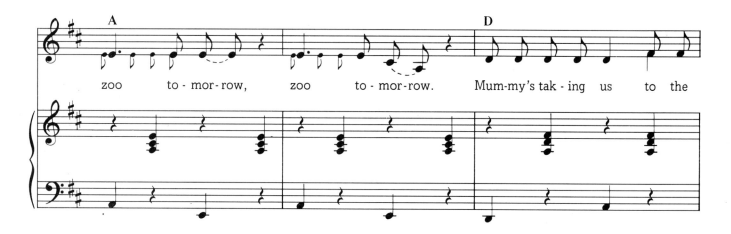

zoo, zoo, zoo. How a-bout you, you, you? You can come

too, too, too, We're go - ing to the zoo, zoo, zoo.

1,2,3.

4. zoo, zoo, zoo. We're go - ing to the

D.S. al ⊕

⊕ Coda zoo, zoo, zoo.

2. Look at all the monkeys swinging in the trees,
   Swinging in the trees, swinging in the trees.
   Look at all the monkeys swinging in the trees,
   We can stay all day.
   Chorus

3. Look at all the crocodiles swimming in the water,
   Swimming in the water, swimming in the water.
   Look at all the crocodiles swimming in the water,
   We can stay all day.
   Chorus

4. Repeat 1st. verse.
   Chorus twice.

Goodnight, Irene

Words and music by Huddie Ledbetter and John A. Lomax.
Adapted lyrics by Raffi and D. Pike.

Fox - es sleep in the for - est, _____ li - ons sleep in their dens. _____ Goats sleep on the moun - tain side and pig - gies sleep in pens. _____

Chorus

I - rene, good night,_____ I - rene, good night._____ Good

night, I - rene, good night, I - rene, I'll

see you in my dreams._____

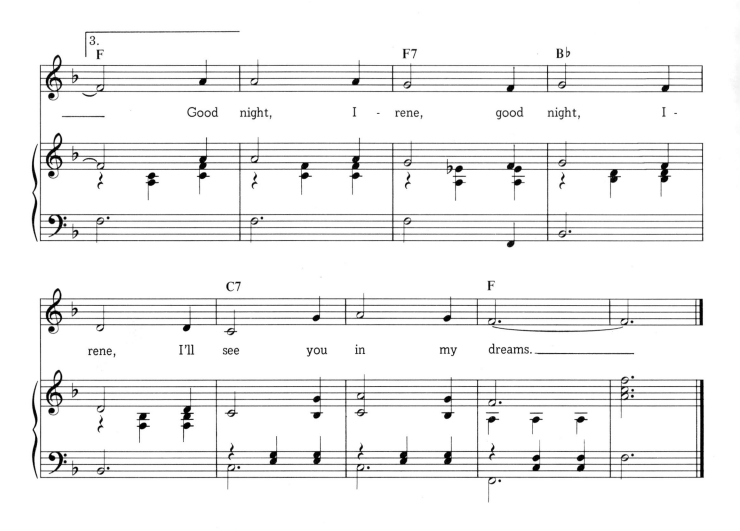

Good night, I - rene, good night, I-
rene, I'll see you in my dreams. _____

2. Whales sleep in the ocean,
   Zebras sleep on land.
   Hippos sleep by the river-side
   And camels sleep on sand.
   Chorus

3. Coyote sleeps in the canyon,
   A birdie sleeps in a tree.
   And when it's time for me to rest,
   My bed's the place for me.
   Chorus

Here Sits A Monkey

Traditional

Oh, Here { sits / lies / plays } a mon-key { in the / under the / by the } chair, chair, chair. { He / He lost all the true loves / She } { He / He had last year, So / She }

rise up on your feet and greet the first you meet, The

hap - pi - est one I know.

Oh,

know.

KELLY

I Wonder If I'm Growing

Words and music by Raffi

GILLIAN

Moderate

I won-der if I'm grow-ing, I won-der if I'm grow-ing. My Mum says yes, I'm grow-ing, but it's hard for me to

see. My Mum says eat your sand-wich, it-'ll make you grow up tall, But when I eat my sand-wich, I'm hard-ly big-ger at all. And I see. My Mum says, "Wash your hands now,

42

Frum troytt
toroffi

If I Had A Dinosaur

Music by Raffi
Words by
Raffi, D. Pike, B. & B. Simpson

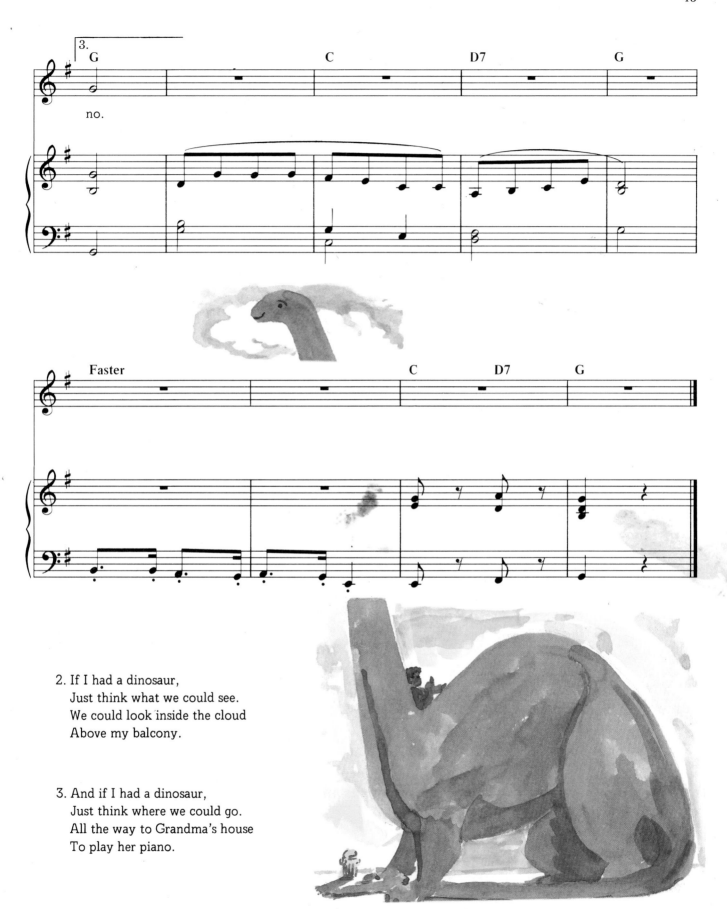

2. If I had a dinosaur,
   Just think what we could see.
   We could look inside the cloud
   Above my balcony.

3. And if I had a dinosaur,
   Just think where we could go.
   All the way to Grandma's house
   To play her piano.

Jig Along Home

Words and music: Woody Guthrie

Medium fast

I went to a dance and the an-i-mals came, Jay-bird danced with horse-shoes on, Grass-hop-per danced till he fell on the floor,___

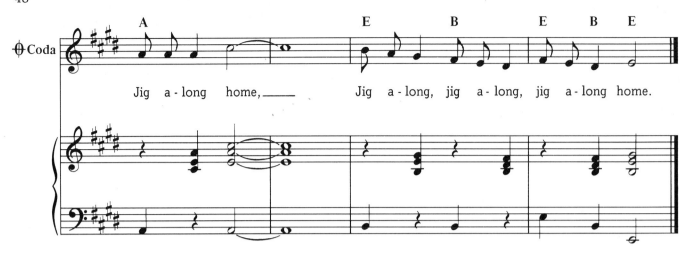

Coda

Jig a - long home,_____ Jig a - long, jig a - long, jig a - long home.

2. Fishing worm danced the fishing reel,
   Lobster danced on the peacock's tail,
   Baboon danced with the rising moon,
   Jig along, jig along, jig along home.
                    Chorus

3. Mama rat took off her hat,
   Shook the house with the old tom cat.
   The alligator beat his tail on the drum,
   Jig along, jig along, jig along home.
                    Chorus

4. The boards did rattle and the house did shake,
   The clouds did laugh and the world did quake,
   New moon rattled some silver spoons,
   Jig along, jig along, jig along home.
                    Chorus

5. The nails flew loose and the floors broke down,
   Everybody danced around and round.
   The house came down and the crowd went home,
   Jig along, jig along, jig along home.
                    Chorus

Listen To The Horses

Words and music
by David Eddleman

fair. Gon - na ride my pal - o - mi - no. Ride him to the fair.

HOWARD

The More We Get Together

Traditional

Waltz tempo

more we get to - geth - er, to - geth - er, to - geth - er, The

Mr. Sun

Traditional

Medium fast *(Whistle 2nd time)*

Oh Mis - ter Sun, Sun, Mis - ter Gol - den sun, please shine down on me. Oh Mis - ter Sun, Sun, Mis - ter Gold - en Sun, hid - ing be - hind a tree.

55

Must Be Santa

Words and music
by Hal Moore and Bill Fredericks

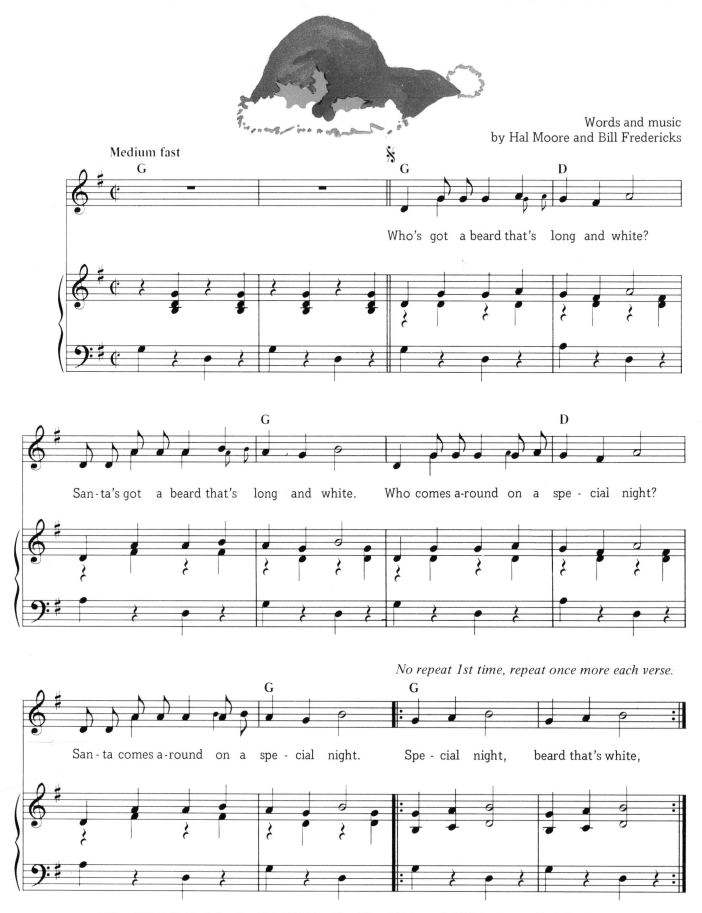

Who's got a beard that's long and white?

San-ta's got a beard that's long and white. Who comes a-round on a spe-cial night?

No repeat 1st time, repeat once more each verse.

San-ta comes a-round on a spe-cial night. Spe-cial night, beard that's white,

Chorus

Must be San - ta, must be San - ta, Must be

Last time, repeat chorus and take Coda

San - ta, San - ta Claus.

D.S.

Coda

Claus.

2. Who's got boots and a suit of red?
   Santa's got . . .
   Who wears a long cap on his head?
   Santa wears . . .
   Cap on head, suit that's red,
   Special night, beard that's white,
   Chorus

3. Who's got a great big cherry nose?
   Santa's got . . .
   Who laughs this way, "Ho, ho, ho? "
   Santa laughs . . .
   Ho, ho, ho, cherry nose,
   Cap on head, suit that's red,
   Special night, beard that's white,
   Chorus

4. Who very soon will come our way?
   Santa very . . .
   Eight little reindeer pull his sleigh,
   Santa's little . . .
   Reindeer sleigh, come our way,
   Ho, ho, ho, cherry nose,
   Cap on head, suit that's red,
   Special night, beard that's white,
   Chorus twice

My Dreydel

Unaccompanied

I have a lit - tle drey - del, I made it out of clay, And

when it's dry and read - y, my drey - del I will play.

Drey - del, drey - del, drey - del, I made it out of clay,

Drey - del, drey - del, drey - del, my drey - del I will play.

KATHY

Raffi
and
Ken Whiteley
in
Concert

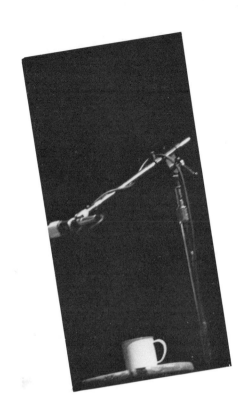

My Way Home

Words and music by Ken Whiteley

lots of things for me to do on my way home, I'll
tell you a few. I can watch a squir-rel climb up a tree, Or
make a buzz like a bum-ble bee, And that's what I might

There are

Chorus

Last time to Coda

do to-day____ on my way home.

home. Yes, that's what I might do to-day___ On

my way home._____

2. When it's pouring rain outside,
   Sometimes I want to stay in and hide,
   But with boots and raincoat I'm okay,
   Splashing in puddles, don't get in my way.
   Chorus

3. When it's cold and snow is on the ground,
   I can go to the hill and slide right down,
   Make a snow angel or build a snowman,
   Have some hot chocolate and do it again.
   Chorus

4. And when it's hot I'm in sneakers and shorts,
   I can play tag or build some forts.
   I can walk alone or with my friends,
   Making up a song that never ends.
   Chorus twice

New River Train

With bounce

Traditional

Rid - ing on that new riv - er train,

rid - ing on that new riv - er train, It's the

same old train _____ that brought __ me __ here, And

gon - na take me back a gain.

It's the same old train that brought me

here, And gon - na take me back a gain.

2. Darlin' you can't love one . . .
   You can't love one 'cause it isn't any fun . . .

3. Darlin' you can't love two . . .
   You can't love two and still be true . . .

4. Honey you can't love three . . .
   You can't love three and still have me . . .

5. Darlin' you can't love Bert . . .
   You can't love Bert if you've lost your shirt . . .

6. 1st verse.

7. Darlin' you can't love Jane . . .
   You can't love Jane if you're insane . . .

8. 1st verse.

9. Darlin' you can't love them all . . .
   The skinny and the fat, the short and the tall . . .

10. 1st verse.

DANIEL

Oh Me, Oh My

EMMA

Words and music by Raffi

don't need an el - e-phant to tie my shoe. No, you don't need an

el - e-phant to tie your shoe, Oh me,— song

2. Oh me, oh my! What'll I do? I can't find a lumberjack to pour my milk.
   But I know what, and so do you. I don't need a lumberjack to pour my milk.
   No, you don't need a lumberjack to pour your milk.

3. Oh me, oh my! What'll I do? I can't find a dinosaur to eat me up,
   But I know what, and so do you. I don't need a dinosaur to eat me up.
   No, you don't need a dinosaur to eat you up.

4. Oh me, oh my! What'll I do? I don't have a radio to sing a song.
   But I know what, and so do you. I don't need a radio to sing a song.
   No, you don't need a radio to sing a song.

Old McDonald Had A Band

Traditional
Adapted and arranged
by Raffi & Ken Whiteley

— — there, Here a —, there a —, ev-'ry-where a — —,

Chorus

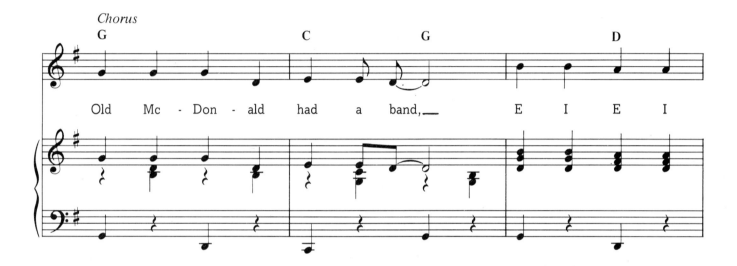

Old Mc - Don - ald had a band,___ E I E I

(Repeat chorus slowly to end.)

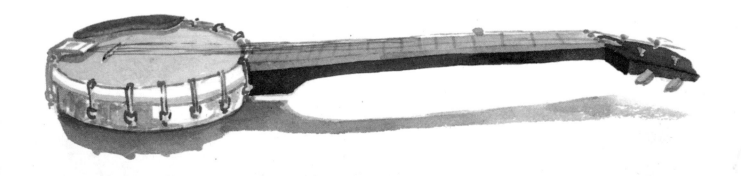

1.-5. | 6.

D.S. | Fine

O. And O.

Peanut Butter Sandwich

Music Traditional
Adapted lyrics by Raffi

Les Petites Marionettes

Traditional

Ain - si font, font, font, les pe -

tites ma - ri - o - net - tes, ain - si font, font, font, trois p'tits

tours et puis s'en vont. Ain - si vont.

Pick A Bale O'Cotton

Words and music by Huddie Ledbetter
(Collected and adapted by John A. Lomax & Alan Lomax)

2. Me and my gal gonna pick a bale o'cotton . . .
   Me and my gal gonna pick a bale a day . . .
   Chorus

3. Peter and Tara gonna pick a bale o'cotton . . .
   Cindy and Franco gonna pick a bale o'cotton . . .
   Chorus

4. Repeat 1st verse.
   Chorus

POPCORN

Words by
Bonnie Simpson and Debi Pike

You put the oil in the pot

And you let it get hot

You put the popcorn in

And start to grin

Sizzle sizzle sizzle sizzle

Sizzle sizzle sizzle sizzle

Sizzle sizzle sizzle sizzle

!POP!

Robin In The Rain

Words and music
by Claire Senior Burke

From Scissors and Songs, Part 2

Shake My Sillies Out

Music by Raffi
Words by Bert and Bonnie Simpson

Got-ta shake, shake, shake my sil-lies out, Shake, shake, shake my sil-lies out, Shake, shake, shake my sil-lies out And wig-gle my wag-gles a-way. 2. Got-ta way, And wig-gle my wag-gles a-way.

2. Gotta clap, clap, clap my crazies out,
Clap, clap, clap my crazies out,
Clap, clap, clap my crazies out,
And wiggle my waggles away.

3. Gotta jump, jump, jump my jiggles out . . .

4. (Slower) Gotta yawn, yawn, yawn my sleepies out . . .

5. Gotta shake, shake, shake my sillies out . . .

The Sharing Song

Words and Music
by Raffi

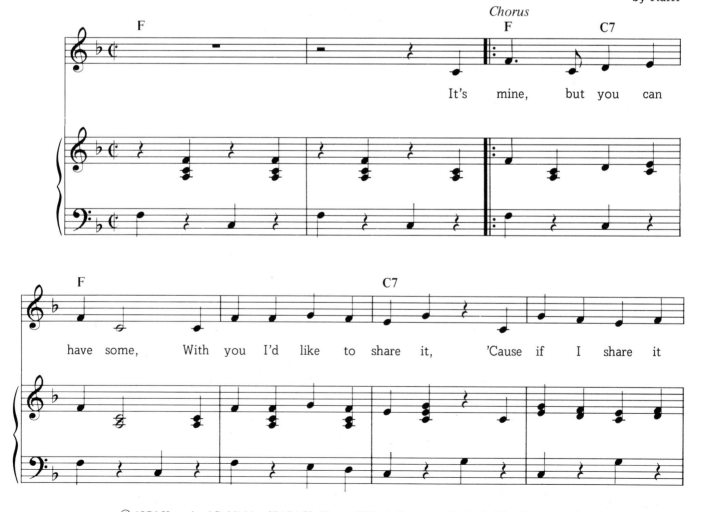

It's mine, but you can have some, With you I'd like to share it, 'Cause if I share it

Six Little Ducks

Traditional

Medium fast

1. 4. Six lit - tle ducks that
2. Down to the riv - er
3. Home from the riv - er

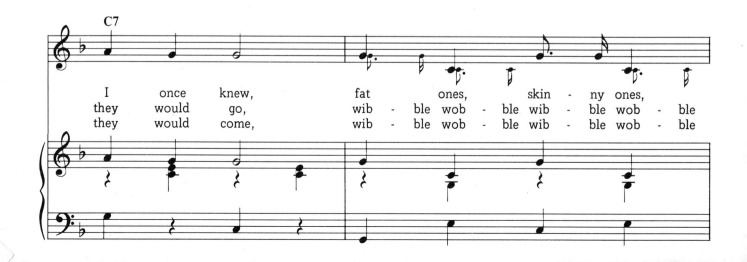

I once knew, fat ones, skin - ny ones,
they would go, wib - ble wob - ble wib - ble wob - ble
they would come, wib - ble wob - ble wib - ble wob - ble

Skin And Bones

Traditional

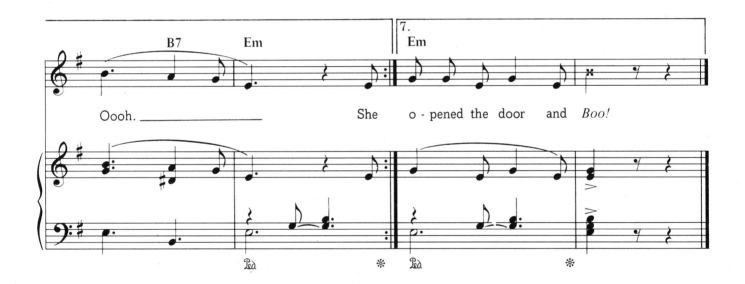

2. She lived down by the old graveyard, Oooh _____

3. One night she thought she'd take a walk, Oooh _____

4. She walked down by the old graveyard, Oooh _____

5. She saw the bones a-layin' round, Oooh _____

6. She went to the closet to get a broom, Oooh _____

7. (last verse above)

Sodeo

Traditional

Medium fast

C

Here we go so-de-o,

so-de-o, so-de-o, Here we go so-de-o, all night long.

G7   C

Step back, Sal-ly, Sal-ly, Sal-ly, Step back, Sal-ly, all night long.   I

G   C

Doc - tor said ___ "Ooh, ah, I got - ta pain in my { side. ___ stomach. ___

Ooh, ah, I got - ta pain in my head." ___ To the front, to the back, to the

see - saw side, ___ To the front, to the back, to the see - saw side, ___ (To the)

D.S. al ⊕
(Omit 2nd time)

Keep repeating and fade out.

⊕Coda

all night long. To the front, to the back, to the see - saw side, ___ To the

Spider On The Floor

Words and music
by Bill Russell

A capella, rubato

There's a   spi - der   on   the   floor,   on   the   floor.   There's a

spi - der   on   the   floor,   on   the   floor.   Who could

ask   for   an - y   more   than   a   spi - der   on   the   floor,   There's a

1.-6. **7.**

spi - der   on   the   floor,   on   the   floor.   Now the   floor.

> Modulate up a semitone with each verse for six verses.
> Spoken phrase after verse 6. Verse 7 in original key.

2. Now the spider's on my leg, on my leg.
   Oh the spider's on my leg, on my leg.
   Oh he's really big! This old spider on my leg.
   There's a spider on my leg, on my leg.

3. Now the spider's on my stomach, on my stomach.
   Oh, the spider's on my stomach, on my stomach.
   Oh, he's just a dumb old lummok, this old spider on my stomach.
   There's a spider on my stomach, on my stomach.

4. Now the spider's on my neck, on my neck,
   Oh, the spider's on my neck, on my neck.
   Oh, I'm gonna be a wreck, I've got a spider on my neck.
   There's a spider on my neck, on my neck.

5. Now the spider's on my face, on my face,
   Oh, the spider's on my face, on my face.
   Oh, what a big disgrace, I've got a spider on my face.
   There's a spider on my face, on my face.

6. Now the spider's on my head, on my head,
   Oh, the spider's on my head, on my head.
   Oh, I wish that I were dead, I've got a spider on my head.
   There's a spider on my head, on my head.

Spoken: But he jumps off

7. Repeat 1st. Verse.

Sur Le Pont D'Avignon

Traditional

Sur le pont d'A - vi - gnon l'on y dan - se, l'on y dan - se,
On the bridge of A - vi - gnon they're all danc - ing, they're all danc - ing,

4 times: French-Piano-English-French

Sur le pont d'A - vi - gnon l'on y dan - se tout en ronde.
On the bridge of A - vi - gnon they're all danc - ing round and round.

Swing Low, Sweet Chariot

Traditional

Chorus

Medium slow

Swing low, sweet char - i - ot,— Com - in' for to car - ry me home, Swing low, sweet char - i - ot,— Com - in' for to car - ry me home. 1. I looked o - ver Jor - dan, and what did I see,— Com - in' for to car - ry me home? I saw a band of an - gels

2. If you get to heaven before I do,
Comin' for to carry me home.
You tell all my friends I'll be comin' there too,
Comin' for to carry me home.

(Chorus take Coda)

There Came A Girl From France

Traditional

Slowly, rubato

There came a girl from France Who did-n't know how to dance. The

on - ly thing that she could do was knees up Moth - er Brown. *(Chorus)* Oh,

Chorus Verse 2, Chorus

knees up Moth - er Brown, knees up Moth - er Brown,
2. Hop - ping on one foot, hop - ping on one foot,

Who Built The Ark

Traditional

Well, who built the ark? No-ah, No-ah.

Who built the ark? Broth-er No-ah built the ark. No-ah built the ark.

1. Did-n't old No-ah build the ark? He

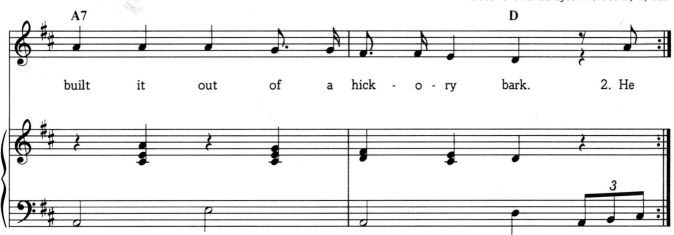

D.S. to chorus after verses 2, 6, 12.

built it out of a hick - o - ry bark. 2. He

He built it long, both wide and tall,
Plenty of room for the large and small.
  Chorus

Now in came the animals two by two,
Hippopotamus and kangaroo.

Now in came the animals three by three,
Two big cats and a bumblebee.

Now in came the animals four by four,
Two through the window and two through the door.

Now in came the animals five by five,
Five little sparrows doin' the jive.
  Chorus

Now in came the animals six by six,
The elephant laughed at the monkey's tricks.

Now in came the animals seven by seven,
Four from home and the rest from heaven.

Now in came the animals eight by eight,
Some were on time and the others were late.

Now in came the animals nine by nine,
Some were shoutin' and some were cryin'.

Now in came the animals ten by ten,
Five black roosters and five black hens.

Now Noah says, "Go and shut that door,
The rain's started dropping and we can't take more."
  Chorus twice.

Willoughby, Wallaby, Woo

Words: Dennis Lee
Music: Larry Miyata

Adapted lyrics by Raffi

From Alligator Pie

Workin' On The Railroad

Traditional

I've been work-in' on the rail - road, all the live - long day.

I've been work-in' on the rail - road, just to pass the time a - way.

Can't you hear the whis-tle blow - ing, rise up so ear-ly in the morn. (*in the morn*)

Y'a Un Rat

Traditional

Polka tempo

Y'a un rat

dans le gren - ier. J'en - tends le chat qui miau - le.

Y'a un rat dans le gren - ier. J'en - tends le chat miau -

ler. J'en - tends J'en - tends, J'en -

tends le chat qui miau - le, j'en - tends, j'en -

2nd time piano plays alone until chorus.

tends, j'en - tends le chat miau - ler. ler.

You Gotta Sing

Traditional

2. You gotta shout . . .
3. You gotta play . . .

4. You gotta hum . . .
5. You gotta sing . . .

You'll Sing A Song And I'll Sing A Song

Words and music: Ella Jenkins

You'll sing a song, And I'll sing a song, And we'll sing a song to-geth - er.

You'll sing a song, and I'll sing a song, In warm or win-try weath - er.

er. er, In warm or win-try weath - er.

2. You'll play a tune, and I'll play a tune . . .　　　3. You'll whistle a tune, and I'll whistle a tune . . .

4. You'll sing a song, and I'll sing a song . . .

Les Zombis Et Les Loups-Garous

Words and music by Bill Russell

1. Madame Zombi elle est méchante *(echo)*
   Mais sa sœur est plus méchante *(echo)*
   Oui, sa sœur est plus méchante *(echo)*
   Mais sa mère est la plus méchante *(echo)*
   Chorus twice

2. Le loup-garou il est sauvage
   Mais son frère est plus sauvage
   Oui, son frère est plus sauvage
   Mais son père est le plus sauvage.
   Chorus twice

SONGS BY ALBUM INDEX

A NOTE TO BEGINNER PLAYERS

Here are some songs that are easy to play because they only have a few chord changes:

Aikendrum
Baa Baa Black Sheep
Bumping Up and Down
Cluck Cluck Red Hen
Down By The Bay
Jig Along Home
The More We Get Together

My Dreydel
Old McDonald Had A band
Pick A Bale O'Cotton
Shake My Sillies Out
Six Little Ducks
Sodeo
Y'A Un Rat

A NOTE ON KEY CHANGES

"THERE CAME A GIRL FROM FRANCE"

Guitar players: By putting a capo behind the third fret and playing in the key of G, you'll be playing the song in its actual key signature.

For the chords	Bb	Eb	F	G7	C	F	G
substitute	G	C	D	E7	A	D	E

" THE CORNER GROCERY STORE"

You may wish to play this song in the key of G.

For the chords	F	C	Bb	G7	Gm
substitute	G	D	C	A7	Am

"GOING ON A PICNIC"

If you want to sing this song in a lower key, try the key of E or F.

For	G	Em	C	D
In the key of E: Play	E	E6	A	B7
In the key of F: Play	F	Dm	Bb	C

"OH ME, OH MY"

I play this with a capo behind the 4th fret in the C formation.

For the chords	E	B	A	F#
substitute	C	G	F	Dm

GUITAR CHORDS

Any string with an "X" over it should not be played.

A
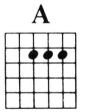

Am
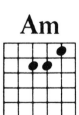

A7
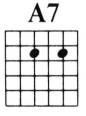

Am7
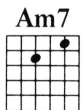

B
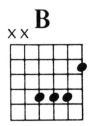

Bm

B7
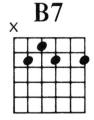

Bm7

Bb
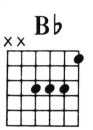